New Zealand in three weeks

About Author

Hello and welcome to my e-book! Im, Thomas, a 30 something from the UK, who in 2015 decided to say goodbye to my mundane career and travel around the world with my Wife. Since then I have explored the most incredible locations, discovering secret places that most tourists haven't even heard of . My goal is to make people realise that travelling is everyone you don't need to be wealthy to explore.

Trust me if you are thinking about exploring New Zealand then do not hesitate. This place has it all, from culture, wildlife, adventure and of course the famous dramatic New Zealand scenery.

In this e-book, I will share my inside tips on what to try while you're in New Zealand and give you a day by day itinerary of the perfect three week trip. Oh and please don't worry, three weeks is a nice amount of time to soak up all things Kiwi!

New Zealand in Three Weeks

So you have booked three weeks holiday and you're planning your trip to New Zealand. Don't worry 3 weeks is a good amount of time and with my guide you will experience the best of New Zealand whilst maximizing every day and yes New Zealand really is as good as they say it is!

To start, we would advise spending 1 week in the North Island and 2 weeks in the South Island and that you most definitely need to hire a camper van! To maximize your time I also advise to fly into Auckland and out of Christchurch. Even though the less touristy North Island is just as beautiful in itself, it goes without saying, the South Island has many more attractions to enjoy, especially when on a 3 week time frame.

Week one overview:

Auckland –> Hobbiton –> Rotorua –> Tongariro Crossing –> Wellington

Week two overview:

Picton –> Abel Tasman -> St Arnaud and Nelson Lakes –> Pancake Rocks –> Fox Glacier and Franz Joseph

Week three overview:

Wanaka –> Queenstown –>Milford Sounds –> Mount Cook –> Christchurch

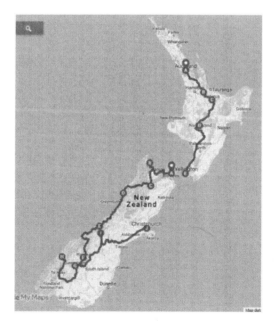

Courtesy of Google Maps

Week 1: The North Island

Day one: Auckland

Morning and Afternoon: A great way to explore Auckland's' harbour is to ride the ferry over to Rangitoto Volcanic Island. There are 3 ferries which depart during the morning with the last leaving around 12:15. So be sure to make it an early start to make the most of the day. The journey takes around 30 minutes, with the last ferry from Rangitoto leaving at 3:30pm. The ferry ride itself is worth the money with its breath taking views and the island is an absolute gem. Most people visit Waiheke Island making Rangitoto a much quieter place away from the tourists. There are various walks you can enjoy on the Island, check them out here.

Evening: Visit the Sky Tower. Located in the heart of Auckland's vibrant city centre, the Sky Tower gives you the perfect opportunity to enjoy the sun setting over the amazing sky line. Tickets are often hard to purchase on the day so it may be a good idea to book before arriving. Click here to check latest deals.

Day 2: Hobbiton as the sun goes down

A long drive from early morning to early afternoon down will see you arrive in Mata Mata south of Auckland and the home of Bilbo, Frodo! If you're a fan of The Lord of the Rings or the Hobbit and let's be honest, who isn't? Then while in New Zealand this is a must do! I didn't know what to expect when arriving here but what a magical place this is. When deciding on buying tickets to Hobbiton, we would suggest buying tickets for the evening. Paying the extra is worth it as you get to have a feast Green Dragon Pub (the Hobbits local watering hole) and a night tour of the set. It will certainly be a highlight of your trip. Check out Hobbiton prices here.

Day 3 and 4 – Rotorua's Geothermal Wonderland and the Tamaki Mouri Village

Another early start to arrive in Rotorua. The reason Rotorua is famous, is of course for its natural hot springs due to its high geothermal activity. This brings a high amount of visitors in the summer months but during the off-peak season, its nice a quiet. The best place to experience the geothermal activity is without a doubt the Wai-O-tapu Thermal Wonderland. Here you will find active geysers, natural coloured hot springs, bubbling mud pits (weirdly mesmerizing), massive volcanic craters and more! Great day out and really interesting. Check out the prices here.

For the evening we would recommend the Tamaki Mauri village. To start, you arrive by coach to the village, here your instantly taken back in time to when the native Mauri people lived. You are greeted with a traditional Mauri welcome (once again terrifying) and then taken through to the village where you're shown how the Mauri's used to live, with the chance to learn the Hakka (although my attempt looked more like Macarena). After a really enjoyable tour of the village, you're then asked to take a seat in the restaurant to fill you belly's with a special prepared traditional Mauri feast. To finish the awesome evening, the Mauri chief and his family display an impressive performance including the Hakka, so get your cameras at the ready! Check out Tamaki Mauri Village here.

Day 5: Tongariro National Park

A couple of hours drive from Rotorua you will arrive at the Tongariro National Park. The most obvious trek to do is the Tongariro Cross Great Walk, and this is exactly what we would advise. This walk is simply awesome and there is no wonder why this is voted the best one day walk in New Zealand!

The 7-8 hour hike takes in views of three volcanoes: Tongariro, Ruapehu (Mount Doom) and Ngauruhoe. If you have enough time and you can opt to climb Ruapehu as part of the walk. The view from the top across the Tongariro is superb and you can even see Mount Tarnaki on the North Island. This adds at least 3 hours onto the overall time but worth the effort. If you're an inexperienced climber please note that most of the mountain is made of scree making it difficult to hold a footing. So please be careful when coming down and watch out for loose rocks rolling past. For up to date information on the crossings accessibility please always check the official DOC website here when planning.

Day 6: Windy Wellington

After an early (3.5 hour) drive from Tongariro, you will arrive in Wellington for lunch time. Wellington has a range of things to do and see but given you only have a day, we would suggest to head straight to the Te Papa Museum. Here you can spend 2 hours or a full day and what's more it's completely free. A superb museum encompassing everything about New Zealand. Personally we visited the museum for 5 hours and found this to be enough.

Parking at the Te Papa Museum is perfect for our camper van as you can stay for 24 hours for a reasonable price. Meaning you can sleep right in the centre of Wellington very cheaply, with everything at your feet.

For the evening, take a walk in the city centre. Wellington is a very cool place to be, with its hipster coffee culture, bars and restaurants you will be spoilt for choice on where to spend the evening.

Day 7: Ferry to Picton

In the morning, take the car ferry over to Wellington to Picton. Believe me when I say that this ferry ride is like non other and has been voted the best in the world. As you leave Wellington Harbour you take in the incredible Cook Straight, then onto the famous Marlborough Sounds where you will find amazing turquoise waters with green hills and a dolphin or two if you're lucky.

For the ferry crossing you have a choice of two main providers, these are Blue Bridge and Interislander. These companies are pretty similar and do the same job but the prices are usually different depending on what offers are available and what type of size your camper is. Check out the Interislander websites here and the Blue Bridge here.

Day 8: Abel Tasman

As you will aware the Abel Tasman is one of the many gems in the South Island and is the home of the Tasman Great Walk. This walk is technically a "two-day hike" but ignore this and save yourself time and money by doing this in one day. The walk itself is easy "there and back" with no hard sections, hugging the coastline. The terrain is cliff top, forestry and board walks and takes around 10 hours (we took it easy). The views are beautiful, so have your camera at the ready.

Day 9: St Arnaud and Nelson Lakes

One of New Zealand's hidden gems in our books. While a lot of people use this road as a means to get to the coast, make sure you stop off for a day in St Arnaud. This is a place with views worthy of any postcard. For information on our day hike click here.

Day 10: Pancake Rocks and Hokitika

Today is a relaxing drive through the country side of nelson lakes to the coast where you will find the awesome Pancake Rocks. A popular tourist spot, but it's worth putting up the hive of people. The coastal attraction is free with a nice path taking you around the rocks that are stacked literally like pancakes. Pretty cool place to enjoy for a couple of hours.

Hokitika itself is a small township on the coast with a nice beach and the now famous HOKITIKA sign made from drift wood. The best attraction in here is most definitely Hokitika gorge which is around 20 min's inland. The gorge itself is popular with photo loving tourists taking snaps of the turquoise river.

Day 11 and 12: Fox Glacier and Franz Joseph

Early drive today to arrive at Franz Josef. Famous
for the Glacier, Franz Josef will not disappoint.
Most people will take the popular (easy) route to see
the glacier. But if you like us, you like to be work a
bit harder for a better view then take the longer
route off the beaten path. This is clearly marked
once you arrive and is about 3 hours round trip.
After your visit Franz Josef, drive to the Fox
Glacier area to set up camp for the night. Parking is
limited here and accommodation is few and far
between, personally we managed to freedom camp
on some public land but were lucky, so plan in
advance.

In the morning, rise early to beat the crowd. The
Glacier itself is probably the lease impressive of the
two but still pretty cool. Over the past two decades
the glacier has receded massively, all the more
reason to appreciate the view right?

Early afternoon it's time to make a detour towards
the Lake Matherson, around 20 min's away off the
main highway. For us this was the best part of the
Glacier region, a 2 hour walk around the lake gives
you incredible views of Fox Glaciers in all its
splendour. You will want to take your time getting
the perfect shot as this lake is so dark it gives the
perfect mirror reflection of the mountain. After the
Lakes we suggest you drive to Wanaka 3 hours
south to arrive early evening.

Day 13 and 14: Wanaka

Roys Peak hike is one of the most rewarding hikes you will ever do. The views of half way up this steep walk are incredible. As this walk is so popular, it's a good idea to get up before sunrise and drive around 20 mins out of Wanaka and find a parking space as these go pretty fast. The walk itself is around 5-6 hours in total but this is well worth the effort. Check out my top ten alternative hikes in New Zealand for more information on Roys Peak.

In the evening you need to visit the boutique cinema of Wanaka. https://www.paradiso.net.nz/

Week Three: The South Island

Day 15 and 16: Queenstown

A little over 1 hour drive south is Queenstown. For the morning we recommend the Frisbee course in the Pine forest park, this is heaps of fun. To do so, walk into town and rent out a couple of Frisbee's for around $10-15 and play the full 18 holes.

In the afternoon it's time for you to let go of your fears and treat yourselves to something you have never experienced before! Queenstown is home of the worlds best extreme activities and you are spoilt for choice. We personally opted for paragliding which was an incredible experience. Definitely book your activity here.

The next day is a hiking day and trust me its a good one! The Ben Lomond track is an 8 hour hike with a steep incline taking in amazing views across the mountainous region and for us one of best views we ever had! If you are lucky you may even come across a Kia or two at the top of the peak. For more information on the track click here.

After your long days hike, it's now time to treat yourselves to the famous Fergburger joint. The portions are pretty big even for my huge appetite.

Day 17 and 18: Milford Sound

Today you have 3.5 hour drive to the incredible Milford Sound and its certainly worth it. The famous fiords of the sounds is home to Hector Dolphins, Bottle Nose Dolphins, Seals and Penguins. There are a number of tour providers and personally we opted for the Juicy cruise. Check out discounted deals here.

The next day be sure to visit the Key Summit track. This a pretty easy 3 hour hike with breath taking views to enjoy. Take your time and relax, remember this is what New Zealand is all about.

After your hike, take the scenic drive back to Queenstown and set up camp for the night.

Day 19 & 20: Mount Cook

3 Hours north of Queenstown is Mount Cook national park. Today is a full day of trail walking to explore the magnificent area of natural beauty. The first hike is the Hooker Valley track which takes around 3 hours. After the easy walk head over to the DOC center where you will find the museum showing the history of the area. We spent around two hours in here.

For the second day we recommend the Sealy Tarns walk. This walk takes around 3 hours and a word of warning, this is pretty tiring. The walk is mainly steps (2000 plus), but the reward you get once you reach the view point is spectacular. We spent around an hour at the top enjoying the view whilst having lunch. In the afternoon its now time to visit the Tasman Glacier. Situated around 15 mins drive from the Mount Cook village, this is an easy 1 hour return walk taking in the glacier and the blue lakes.

Day 21: Christchurch and Flight Home

If you have time on the day of your flight, you have
two options. One, venture into the city or Two, visit
the Banks Peninsula / Akaroa. The inner city of
Christchurch is yet to rebuild from the devastating
earthquake of 2011, making it a very interesting
ghost town. Within the city, the Kiwis have created
an oasis type high street using colourful steel
shipping containers. The people of New Zealand
won't let an earthquake stop their creatively, that's
for sure.

Thank you for reading my quick guide. I hope you enjoy New Zealand as much as I did. Please follow my Instagram page thom.marsden for more inspiration on your next trip.

Printed in Great Britain
by Amazon

35609986R00015